RISING FROM THE ASHES

HOW I TOOK CONTROL OF MY LIFE

RISING FROM THE ASHES

How I Took Control of My Life.

Written by Billy J Brown II
Alabama

Printed in The United States of America

All Rights Reserved

Edited by: Becki Lee Chiasson

Copyright Page

ISBN-13: 978-1463784195

Contact Billy J Brown for your corporate event

www.Billyjbrown.com

Facebook: Billy J Brown Inspires You

or Contact him at

888-586-7381

Email: inspireyouproductions@gmail.com

RISING FROM THE ASHES

Table of Contents

Introduction

Rising From The Ashes

The book before you is a journey from tragedy to victory and shows you that all things are possible with vision and determination.

This book is dedicated to my family and friends for their support in my journey through the years and most important to Jesus our savior.

Chapter 1 ➤

It is July 7, 1974 as my family of seven travels from rural Alabama back to Houston, Texas from a great 4th of July holiday with family. It is dark on Hwy 90 in rural Grand Bay, Alabama as we cross over the state line into Mississippi. We didn't know what lay ahead that would change the direction of our lives forever.

Mom (Fleecy) and dad (Billy Joe Sr) were in the front seat of our old 1960 station wagon and Aunt Betty and Uncle Robert sat in the back seat chatting.

Myself at the age of two, just two weeks shy of being three, was asleep alongside my 2-year-old cousin William and my 4-year-old sister Ramona. As the car moved past a weighing station the family decided to stop at a gas station for a break, that's when it all changed as an 18-wheeler was coming in the same path with the driver asleep at the wheel. He had driven for days high on speed to get the load where it needed to be.

The adults heard the metal of the car being impacted and the slamming of the car into a ditch without warning. Smoke began to fill the car as they climbed out the windshield to safety. The gas tank had been ruptured and the left side of my body was now lying in the gas tank that was burning. Ramona jumped up from the noise and an unknown African-American man broke out a window to rescue her to safety but the flames started to consume the car and myself and cousin William.

The family tried with effort to get to us with no results as we were trapped in the car with the fire; thank God we remained asleep from the smoke which allowed us to escape the pain that our bodies must have been feeling.

My mom rushed to the 18-wheeler asking for his fire extisher so that she could save us and the driver refused as he said it was too late and he didn't want to have to buy another one.

Sirens were heard in the background as the Mobile Fire Department and local volunteers showed up to help as the fire raged out of control. William was brought to safety by the fireman but they told my family that it was too late for me as I was lying in the fuel tank that was on fire and they couldn't get to me. My mom took a stand that would save me as she told them, "I don't care what you do, get me my baby now!" The fireman made a way to me somehow and as they climbed out of the ditch the car exploded. I had 3rd degree burns over 65% of my body.

As I was being rolled on a stretcher to the awaiting Coast Guard Helicopter I remember waking up and seeing all the water and fire hoses and was trying to see what was going on. God had given a sense of peace and calm over my mind and body as I felt no pain.

Myself, William and Ramona were airlifted to Singing River Hospital so that treatment could begin.

Ramona had some flash burns that required a few days in the hospital then some at-home treatment, which cleared up her burns in a few weeks.

Rising from the Ashes

William had 3rd degree burns on about 30% of his body so he and I would be in for a long rehab from this.

I would spend the next 9 months learning how to walk again and use my hands with fingers missing

The Choice

I recall this moment as if it was today as time stood still while I was in the burning car and God was with me talking about helping man for the greater good. I saw the accident from an outside- looking-in viewpoint as God showed me what was taking place and asked me if I wanted to be spared or suffer for the greater good of mankind. I feel that we all make decisions in life that affect us down the road that at the time we don't understand but God has a greater plan and I chose to follow his plan.

Later in the years I was able to share with my family images from the accident that only people on the outside of the car saw or heard which proved to be that what I remembered was real.

I saw the burns as a curse during my years of growing up but I will share later in this book how I recalled the event between me and God in the car.

Rising from the Ashes

I will instruct you
and teach you in
the way you
should go, I will
counsel you and
watch over you.

- Psalm 32:8

Rising from the Ashes

As I lay in Singing River the doctors told my mom I had only hours to a few days left to live as the burns covered my face, head, arms, back and lower legs. They advised her to keep me comfortable and take me out to see the ducks beside the hospital's pond. I remember that day like it was yesterday as I fed the ducks with my hands all wrapped up, smiling at them as they seemed so happy to see me.

The next day things got bad as gangrene set up in my body, which is an infection that wasn't curable, and it would cause my death if drastic action wasn't taken.

My mom was 20 years old and had to make the hardest decision of her life and that was to allow them to amputate four fingers from my left hand.

I recall that afternoon as they came in and gave me a shot in my thigh, which caused me to cry and gave me a fear of needles that lasted until my late teens. They rolled me into the ER and I wasn't sure what was taking place at the time until I came out and I felt pain in my hand and I cried, "Momma, they stole my fingers."

I didn't understand why they did what they did at the time. As weeks went by, I was unable to walk and nobody knew why until I was airlifted to Jackson Medical Center in Jackson, Mississippi and they discovered that my hip was dislocated.

Rising from the Ashes

After a few weeks the family got a call from the local Shriners Chapter offering to take us into their care and give us free medical treatment at their Galveston, Texas hospital as the family had no medical coverage at the time.

I would spend the next seven months at Galveston Shrine Burn Center getting the care that I needed both physically and mentally.

The care started by soaking in hot water with bleach as they scrubbed your skin to get the new skin to grow which caused a great deal of pain as pain killers were not used in the 70's like they are today.

Skin grafts would be a big part of my life for the next 17 years and the burn area had to be covered with skin from other parts of my body to allow new skin to grow.

I had to relearn to walk and to write and feed myself again. There was a time I sat and gave myself food with my toes because my hands were bandaged up.

As I returned home from the eight months in the hospital I didn't know I was any different than the other kids and I showed it by playing like the other kids and just living life to the fullest. My mom said she would never let me feel sorry for myself and feel any different than any other kid.

Most summers consisted of trips to the burn center for additional care and surgeries. I would guess that I have had close to 75-80 operations over the 17-year period.

Rising from the Ashes

During this time the accident tore my family apart as my dad turned to alcohol to dull his pain and my mom was left to take care of us herself, which she was glad to do.

I remember my dad trying to take me from the hospital bed and kidnap me because of the possible financial gain from the accident.

As a kid I grew up always scared that he was going to be in my closet trying to get me.

All I wanted was for my dad to be there for us but he never was. My mom played the role of Father and Mother to our family.

Rising from the Ashes

Don't wait. The
time will never be
just right.
Napoleon Hill

Rising from the Ashes

Questions to Ask yourself

- What fires have I had in my life?

- What scars did it leave me with?

- What did I learn?

  - What would I change about that event?

Congratulations on finishing Chapter 1 and getting to think about events in your life. I look forward to your growth in the following chapters.

Rising from the Ashes

Chapter 2

My Journey Through the years

Throughout my young life there were many obstacles that I had to overcome to be able to function as a normal person in life. It was very surprising to me when my mom would take me into a supermarket how mean some adults could be; they would make remarks like, "How can you take him out in public looking like that?" or state that I looked like a monkey in my burn suit that helped suppress the scars.

I remember the days playing on the beach with close friends Christy, Shawn and cousins and it never hit my mind that I was any different than any other kid.

Early school years came about quickly for me

I remember my first day at kindergarten that was located in First Baptist Church in Bay Minette, Al. I was so excited to have a chance to learn and be around other kids my age to play and grow together in life. School started and I fit right in from day one as most kids knew me from around town and it wasn't a big deal until I moved away some two years later to a small town in Jay, Florida when my mom got married to my stepdad Doug McCurdy. I entered into the 1st grade there and it was a tough adjustment as my stepdad had high standards for us as kids and made us work even harder in the field and around the house of which I'm now grateful because it gave me a great work ethic that would help me in the future.

Rising from the Ashes

As the years go by and as kids age, there comes about different views on what is and isn't accepted in life based on their belief systems. Kids began to pick on me throughout the years, but I never let it hold me back as I pressed on just being me and loving who I was on the inside. I recall the names being said such as

Charcoal Face

Monkey Face, from my wraps I had to wear

Monster

During these years it really started to affect me and my emotions about myself as I saw that people did see me differently now.

The principal at the school called me in during my second grade year and told me and my parents that I had to start wearing a hat as my baldness was an eyesore to some people and was not appropriate; I never understood this since he had no hair. Most the kids were true friends just some weren't.

Middle School and High School

We all know that hormones kick in and who knows what we become during this time as so many things are changing in our lives that we can't figure it all out. We tend to get into groups or cliques to hang out with.

During this time we moved back to the small town of Bay Minette and that is where I took up the love of football, which is like a religion in Alabama.

Rising from the Ashes

We moved into our new home when I was 12, and my life changed one day as I walked outside to watch the telephone guy hook up some wires. We began to talk and Mr. Charles asked me if I ever thought about playing football, and I said, "Ohh yes." Charles said, "That's great because I coach the city football team and would love to have you play with us." Within a week I was signed up and ready to play.

I was surrounded by a great group of guys and coaches who didn't treat me any differently than anyone else and I didn't expect them to.

Even then, some teammates had issues with me being different. Some would say, "Hey, he doesn't have all his fingers so I don't want him touching me," so that is the one I would hit the hardest on the next play.

I had a lot of fun playing in the city league so I decided the following year to join the middle school team.

Wow, these guys were tough and fast so I had to work harder than ever to make it. The coaches pushed me to be the best and my teammates helped push me as we grew strong bonds together.

THE PLAY

During my 9th grade year I was on the sideline and our team was playing the Foley Lions for the county championship, as we had been undefeated for the past two years. It was the 4th quarter and the stars of the team were on the field, but Foley started driving with little time on the clock and was running the ball off tackle every play and couldn't be stopped. Coach Shiver and Coach Cabiness

Rising from the Ashes

swapped many defensive tackles into the game to no avail. Then all of a sudden, Coach said, "Put Billy in." At this time I had only played in the secondary covering receivers but liked to play anywhere I could, so I was sent in with one statement: "You're our last hope; we have tried everyone else."

Into the game I went. It was third down and just a few yards and they were within 30 yards of scoring with less than a minute to play.

I lined up against the offensive guard and he looked at me and said, "Look at the freak," and that's all I needed to hear.

The ball snapped and I ran by him unblocked and hit the quarterback who flipped the ball in the air to the running back, who I hit in the chest with my helmet, driving the ball loose. And as I fell on the ball recovering it for our team, time expired and the championship was ours.

Rising from the Ashes

Every person who wins in any undertaking must be willing to cut all sources of retreat. Only by doing so can one be sure of maintaining that state of mind known as a burning desire to win - essential to success. Napoleon Hill

I got involved in several clubs to keep myself busy with life. I did well in school as I really enjoyed my teachers and classes for the most part.

Rising from the Ashes

And during Physical Education, I didn't care if it was basketball, soccer or baseball, I was always up for some rough sports.

I continued playing sports at Baldwin County High School from soccer to Football and we ended the year at 10-0 undefeated and Area Champs and I went on to win the Bryant Jordan athletic achievement award for our area which was a huge honor since the award was names after Bear Bryant. Roll Tide!!!

As I graduated, life was getting tough trying to deal with dating and the job market and I realized that people really do look at me differently in the aspect of, "Well, maybe he has special needs or isn't as good as someone normal."

I remember in college the dating scene was tough. I would go out with the guys and always be the one who girls shied away from, not realizing that it was how I was seeing myself that was causing this. I had depression creeping up on me without even knowing it. This is when depression started to take over my life and affect me both emotionally and phsyicaly.

Love

In 2001 I met the love of my life a girl froma small town in Mobile County Alabama named Melodie, we met online via AOL chat and has a instant connection and startered talking on the phone on a daily basis as a few days went but we traded pics of each other and I loved her sweet smile as you could see the love and passion in her eyes. We set up

Rising from the Ashes

our first date so I was on my way to her house and very nervous about meeting her and the family for the first time.

I'm driving down the road talking with her on the phone as I felt my heart racing as I got closer to her house and she would ask how much longer before you get here. I pulled into the drive and said I will see you in a few seconds. The walk up the driveway seemed like it was a mile long then I reached out and rung the doorbell. The door opended and I saw the most gourgeous person I have ever laid my eyes on. I had her some gifts as I handed it to her she dropped them and we both had a big laugh so that broke the ice. I came in and spent some time chatting with the family like I had known them for years.

It was truly love at first site. Off on the date we went and headed to a local restaurant to eat. We didn't get much food as we were busy chatting so much and she dropped her silverware on the floor which got a big laugh from us both.

We spent everyday together for the next few months and I would say I love you and she would say thank you, I was like well do you love me and finally the words I was waiting for came as she told me I love you! We dated for a year then got engaged and a year later was married and she looked like an angel on our wedding day. After the wedding reception we headed to the honeymoon at Disney world and we had a blast. The day I met Melodie she said you date me you go to church and that changed my life forever. Melodie is truly a blessing from God in my life and brings balance to me.

Firefighter

Rising from the Ashes

I decided to get a career in Fire/Medic work to help give back to the community. This experience helped me grow as a person and come out of my shell as I had to in order to serve the patient who needed me.

Through the year I worked in a major inner city where I got to see a lot of things that most people don't get to see in their lifetime, from drive-bys to multiple house fires at one time set by vagrants or gangs in the area.

I quickly rose through the ranks in our Local Volunteer Fire Department serving at all officer levels and finally as Fire Chief who oversaw 35 guys in our town. What a joy it was to serve with these great guys and what some wonderful times we had with each other throughout the years.

After getting injured a couple of times in my late career I decided it was time to move onto something else in life that would pay more and be a little safer. It still feels good when someone comes up to me in a store and says, "Hey, you're the guy who saved my life."

Real Estate

I took a look at the paper one day at work and saw an ad for real estate school, in which I had some interest, as in the previous years I had some rentals that I purchased and thought it would be a good avenue to make some money.

I took the class and once I passed the test I hit the ground running as a real estate agent and had quick

Rising from the Ashes

success as I wasn't afraid to talk to people and took on anyone to get a listing. Within a few months I had 30 plus listing and the phones were ringing. I would soon find out how sales could be since you didn't have many laws to protect your listing or buyers from other agents. There are many rules but a lot of loopholes for people to get around, and I didn't like the way real estate agents treated each other so unfairly just to make money. But I decided to stay in the game and focused my knowledge on helping people find foreclosures in the area to either buy as a home to live in or to renovate and flip for sale to someone. The timing was right as I started getting a big rolodex of clients who wanted houses and I sold them as quickly as they got them ready. Money to agents is a lot like blood is to sharks in the water; they start to swim around to see what's going on and how they can get into the action. It wasn't long before I started losing clients because agents with listings wouldn't treat my offers fairly and the clients had no choice but to go to them to get any offers accepted for the house they wanted.

I was with a large franchise and rose to be the top agent in the state for them, so they approached me about becoming an owner of a franchise in the area. The person I worked for would make an override on the production I did, which I thought was great because I would make more and the person who brought me in would still make 10% of what I did and get a finder's fee for me buying a franchise.

I found out how quickly you go from the top of the hill and being liked to the bottom and being disliked because you're not bringing all the glory to that person anymore.

Rising from the Ashes

I really looked up to this person as a mentor and was shocked when he turned his back on me and started dragging my name and reputation through the mud, because he built his office on my back throughout the last year.

I pushed on and opened my office with 12 or so agents and we started out on fire until we started to lose listings and agents to the old office, as the owner kept harassing the people and starting rumors that had people scared to work for anyone else but him. It seemed like every 3-4 months we had some type of complaint fielded against us from one of his agents and/or customers, so after we got down to three agents left and our name being trashed in town, we decided to close the franchise and move on to other things and hope the dust would settle.

Over the past three years we had purchased approximately 20 homes valued around 2.5 million dollars, which we rented out or had for sale. We had a good life going and were excited about what was next, so we opened our own independent real estate office just to do our own thing. It did okay through the next year.

Our son is here

We got very excited as our son was on his way and due April 22. It was extra special because we had to go to a doctor to get IVF done to help my wife conceive as she suffers from a cyst problem that keeps her from ovulating.

Rising from the Ashes

April 22 arrived and our son was born which is also my moms birthday which made her very happy. What a miracle it was! We got so excited to have his love in our house and for him to be healthy and strong.

I have been so proud to have a son who looks so perfect and has his mothers smile. The one thing I will remember about his birth is that I got food poisiong the night before and was sick all during the delivery my wife would push and I would get sick, after he was here I was admitted to the hospital for dehydration and was the next day before I got to see my baby boy.

Rising from the Ashes

Chapter 3

Point of No return

THE STORM

Everything seemed to be looking up. August 2005 came and our town got hit by Hurricane Katrina and we lost about half our house in the storm. We didn't have flood insurance and many mortgage companies wanted their money. Hardware and supply stores started suing us and we had zero income coming in. We did a lot of debris cleanup and didn't get paid the over $200,000 we had coming in to us from the work we did, and this did us in.

We met with our attorney and decided that we needed to file bankruptcy since a lot of deals we had on the table had fallen through, and some non-trustworthy employees had taken a lot of money from us.

You quickly find out who your true friends are when something like this happens, as the ones who are about the money leave you holding the bag and the blame. We had friends who we treated as family turn their backs on us and even some church members really hurt us to our core, so we left the church. We closed down our real estate business under pressure from the Real Estate Board, which didn't think I should be selling real estate since I lost some houses in foreclosures, even though some big names in town did the same thing but it was okay for them.

Rising from the Ashes

After losing our home and becoming homeless and living for a short time in an RV park, we knew something had to change.

I recall the repo guy showing up and taking our cars and us having to move out of our home as we had friends and church members suing us for crazy things that didn't matter anymore to us. We tried to make right by people, but we could never give enough; they always wanted more.

I recall seeing my 6-month-old boy and not knowing if I could put diapers on him or feed him because we had lost it all.

I felt so beat down and useless as my life began to spin out of control.

Drinking began to take over my life and I was not making good decisions in my life as I felt that everything I did was wrong and useless.

I felt God didn't love me and my family didn't need me around anymore.

Many nights as I drove around, I thought about just running my car into a tree and ending my pain and the pain I had been causing others in my life.

Rising from the Ashes

Edison failed 10, 000 times before he made the electric light. Do not be discouraged if you fail a few times.
Napoleon Hill

Rising from the Ashes

- **What Storms have you had?**
- **What did it cost you?**
- **How did it make you feel?**

Rising from the Ashes

-I believe we all get to a point in our lives when something has to change for our survival. I reached this point in October 2008 when I'd had enough of being kicked while I was down and knew if I didn't do something there would be no return. I researched around for different seminars and came across a guy by the name of Anthony Robbins who would be speaking in Orlando, Florida in October, so I took what little money I had and purchased a $495 ticket and took a chance.

Day 1: I showed up at the event along with 3,000 other people and was very nervous about the event and not sure what to expect of it. I saw an area that had a sign labeled "special needs area" and I saw people in wheelchairs and on crutches and stuff and it got my attention. I went over to see if I could help with these guys and met some great Tony Robbins crew members who made me feel welcomed and important.

Throughout that day I helped get some people in and out of the event who had special needs. The evening came and there was to be a fire walk where Tony would take people out to 20+ fire lanes for us all to walk on hot coals with our bare feet. I guess you could say I had a great deal of fear about this event.

On the way to the walk I saw a girl trying to push a larger girl and it wasn't working out, so I offered help and began to push her. She couldn't see me well since it was dark out.

Rising from the Ashes

As I began to talk with the woman, who was around 3o, she was telling me about her story and all the ailments that she had that limited her movement. From what I was seeing and hearing, they were more mental limitations she had set in her mind than actual, real problems, so as we came into the light she turned and saw me with burns on my face and one hand with only four fingers and the other with none pushing her through the grass and dirt. She stood up and said, "I will never get in that chair again. I have nothing to fear." WOW! It was at that point a light came on in my mind that I may have a greater purpose at this event than just myself.

As I approached the fire lane, the crew members kept moving me from lane to lane and this was troubling because I was already nervous about fire and was thinking, "Okay, this is a sign to back out and not burn to death." But the greater forces had a great cause as I got shifted to Tony Robbins' line, which would be like the odds of winning the lottery.

When I stepped up to the fire lane, Tony grabbed my shoulder and told me to make my move and get into state, and wow, is he big in person, so I got into state and stormed across the fire lane. At this moment my life would be changed forever; as I crossed over, I saw a beautiful blonde call out to me and tell me to follow her and I was thinking, "Ohh lord, I have burned to death on the fire walk, but hey at least God sent me a beautiful angel to get me." It was Sage Robbins, who is Tony's wife; she wanted me to share my story with them and meet Tony after the event. Tony shared

Rising from the Ashes

that I could affect many people around the world with my story.

I went back the second day and was supercharged to change my life for good. I participated at the event 110% so that I could soak it all in.

I attended a second event just six months later to get recharged and make some minor adjustments to what I heard the first time, and I began to listen to all of Tony's materials and drive them into my soul to make lasting change.

I signed up for coaching with Tony's company so that I could get some direction in life and on my goals. This is when I got a great coach in Darrell, who was assigned to me by Tony's coaching team leader.

When we had our coaching I stated that I wanted to be able to help people and be able to share my story, and one of the things Darrell suggested was to join a speakers training in my area called Toastmasters. This decision will help to reshape my future and has helped shape this book.

I joined up right away and now within the last two years I have risen the ranks in leadership in Toastmasters and have as well become an Advanced Level speaker in the club.

Since this event I have crewed for Tony's event five times and have gone to more of his advanced events to work on my leadership and the direction in my life to be able to help others pursue their dreams, because the one thing I

Rising from the Ashes

wanted in life when I was hurting and down was someone to help me.

Just in the past two years I have been able to share my story with tens of thousands of people from around the world and meet some great role models for myself along the way.

Tony Robbins' event changed my life and I will share with you in the following chapters some things that I did that made a huge impact on my life.

In time of trouble He shall set me upon a rock

- Psalms 27:5

Rising from the Ashes

- What will it take for you to make a change?

- What will you cost if you don't?

- How will it make you feel?

- What will change bring you?

- How does this make you feel now?

Rising from the Ashes

Chapter 4

Rebuilding my Life and How You Can Too

Step one was to rearrange my way of thinking in my mind and I did this by reading every book I could get my hands on so that I could put as much positive stuff in my mind as I could.

These books ranged from Tony Robbins' material to the following.

Think and Grow Rich by Napoleon Hill

The Richest Man in Babylon by George S. Clason

Live Your Best Life Now by Joel Osteen

The 4-Hour Work Week by Timothy Ferriss

The Traveler's Gift by Andy Andrews

Many Zig Ziglar books and saw him in person twice as a speaker.

Why We Want You To Be Rich by Donald Trump and Robert Kiyosaki

Rising from the Ashes

There are many more books that played a huge part in my rebuilding to which I owe a lot.

I took a great quote and wrote in on a sticky note and placed it on my bathroom mirror so that myself and my son could read it each day as we brush our teeth.

"Winners never quit and quitters never win."

Vince Lombardi

This quote was shared at a Toastmasters meeting by a friend R. Roberts and it stuck with me and helps me with the push I need each day.

Many more stickies made their way to my mirror with little sayings such as what I wanted to be so I stated it.

I am a great speaker

I am successful

Rising from the Ashes

Money comes to me nonstop

I am Love

I am Courage

I Love God

God Loves me

I'm a leader

I'm a great Dad

I'm a great Husband

I'm a great Son

I'm a great friend

Rising from the Ashes

A man is but the product of his thoughts what he thinks, he becomes.

Mohandas Gandhi

Rising from the Ashes

After brushing my teeth, it was so important that I start my day in a peak state so I would take the following steps to ensure that.

30 Minutes for Power

I would find a place to have at least 30 minutes to myself so that I could work on this. I would even do it in the car on the way to the office.

If at home, I would light a candle or incense.

I would breathe deep into my belly and hold it in for around 10 seconds to allow the oxygen to fill my lungs and give me energy, then I would breathe out long and hard to push out the old air in my lungs, I would do this routine for around 3-5 minutes and could feel my energy level rise and found myself more aware of my surroundings.

Power Move

I would stand tall with my feet approximately 12 inches apart as Tony had showed us to do at his events. I would act as if an anchor was tied to my feet and would make a power move

Rising from the Ashes

and yell YES, YES, YES! This would make my body begin to radiate energy all over.

I felt this phrase stated how I should prepare for each day:

Whatsoever thy hand findeth to do, do it with all thy might.

- Ecclesiastes 9:10

Visualize

The mind doesn't know the difference between an actual event or a made-up event in your mind's eye. I would close my eyes and see myself going through the day and what actions I would take and how I would handle things as they came up. I would see the end of the day and how I felt, what I heard and the results so that as I went into the day it was as if I had already been there.

Can you imagine going into a meeting or negotiations already having done a

Rising from the Ashes

runthrough in your mind, how much easier it would be?

I also at least once a month sit down and visualize my life in one month, six months and a year to see my goals and the results of my actions in my life and who they have affected and what I feel, which helps me push on.

GOALS

Here are a few statements about why goals are important.

It has been stated in many writings that

"Goals not written are just a wish"

"A goal is a dream with a deadline."
~ Napoleon Hill

"Begin with the end in mind."
~ Stephen Covey

Rising from the Ashes

"What you get by achieving your goals is not as important as what you become by achieving your goals."
~ Zig Ziglar

Setting my goals became a passion because it gave me direction and purpose in life.

What is your purpose in life?

Finding your purpose will push you far more in life than anything else because it gives you something to look at that is bigger than you.

What will you feel when you do this?

You can have great rewards in your life by following your passion and doing the steps needed to achieve the goals as it develops you into a great person.

What will it take?

What will be some steps that you need to take to get the wheels rolling and what will you need to give up to allow it to happen?

Are you willing to let a few things go in life to be able to serve the greater good?

Rising from the Ashes

Every person who wins in any undertaking must be willing to cut all sources of retreat. Only by doing so can one be sure of maintaining that state of mind known as a burning desire to win - essential to success.
Napoleon Hill

Let's work on goal setting now.

We need to work on all areas of our life when it comes to goal setting so that we can be whole and serve at a higher level.

The Wheel or Balance of Life

This will help you take a look at each aspect of your life and see if you have balance or not.

Rising from the Ashes

In my life I had more in one area and less in others which made my wheel hard to balance as I had no balance in my life, so I knew to grow as a person I had to correct this and take action to add balance.

We make choices in life as to what we direct our time to and what to avoid. Life keeps us busy at work, with kids, then we get home and want to relax and we forget the little things like our relationships, personal growth and spirituality.

One of the biggest things we can do is sit down and write out what we can do in each of these areas so that we may grow and prosper to the highest level possible in life and be able to be truly happy with our life and who we affect in it.

Rising from the Ashes

What does your chart look like in your life right now?

What does it need to look like?

Rising from the Ashes

Brain Dump

A great tool that I discovered was to sit down and write out everything that came into my mind that I hadn't done in life that I would enjoy doing. Here are some:

Travel to all 50 states

Speak on stage and get paid

Travel around the world as a speaker

Be active in my community

Coach sports

Have a million dollars in the bank

 Write a Book "Hey good idea, right!"

These are a few that I came up with and what it gave me was a blueprint now to work on my goals and action plans, which really got the brain waves moving. I truly believe that you attract what you desire and think about in life.

Rising from the Ashes

Ask and it will be given to you; seek and you will find; knock and the door will be opened to you

Matthew 7:7

Rising from the Ashes

Action Plan

The action plan is what steps must be taken to have success toward my goals.

This needs to include the following:

1: Specific tasks: What exactly needs to be done.

2: Time deadline: By what time is this task to be completed.

3: What resources are needed: Money, Education or People.

Each time you write a goal, you should write an action plan and do something that day towards your goal to have true results.

Let me show you an example.

I wanted to be a speaker so I wrote this:

1: I needed to sign up with Toastmasters to learn how to speak and would do so by looking them up online.

2: I needed to do this within 30 days.

Rising from the Ashes

3: I would buy a book about public speaking.

As you can see, I wrote the goal and did an action plan followed by what specific task I needed to do, time frame to do it by, and what resource I would employ to help me with this goal.

Results were I got on the internet and located a Toastmasters Club and signed up to attend a meeting. I did this on day one and was at a meeting within 10 days of writing my goal and now I'm doing professional speaking. So you can see that by following my action plan I was able to stay on target.

Always bear in mind that your own resolution to succeed is more important than any other.
Abraham Lincoln

Rising from the Ashes

Daily Diary

I recommend that you keep a diary of your travels so that as you look back you can see the changes in your life and also hold yourself accountable for what you state your goals are in life.

In the diary it is a good idea to write positive affirmations which are statements you write to help your self-esteem and emotions in life by stating what you need to raise your spirits. The more you do this, the better you will become and feel as you ingrain this into your soul.

Examples are:

I'm love

I'm happy

I'm handsome

I'm beautiful

I'm fit

Rising from the Ashes

I'm a great friend

I'm a great husband

I'm a great father

I'm a great mother

I'm smart

I speak well

I'm a great leader

I'm strong

I'm healthy

I have energy

I rise early

I sleep well

I run fast

I share my love easily

I'm spiritual

As you can see, speaking these into your mind will change your life drastically; even if

Rising from the Ashes

you don't feel it yet, you will see the change in your life.

"As you speak so shall you become"

Bruce Lee

Find a Mentor

One of the great resources that most people often forget is to ask for help from people who have gotten to the levels that you aspire to be at in life.

So many times we try and invent the wheel to success, and the smartest man doesn't know everything but knows where to find the answers in life.

Ask someone in business who has been successful what made them that way and what did they learn and what would they do differently if needed now in life.

Ask a happily married couple how they have maintained a happy relationship and tips that you could apply in yours.

Rising from the Ashes

If you don't have that relationship, write down the top ten things you want in a mate as most of us go through life not knowing what we want so we never find it.

Find someone in your local church if you desire to be more spiritual or there are many books and online resources that can direct you in the path that you need to find someone to help you.

One of the great stories that shows the great use of a mentor was in the Bible: the story of Joshua who was mentored by Moses who allowed him to endure to lead his people.

Joshua 1:6-9, "Be strong and courageous, because you will lead these people to inherit the land I swore to their forefathers to give them. Be strong and very courageous. Be careful to obey all the law my servant Moses gave you; do not turn from it to the right or to the left, that you may be successful wherever you go. Do not let this Book of the Law depart from your mouth; meditate on it day and night, so that you may be careful to do everything written in it. Then you will be prosperous and successful. Have I not commanded you? Be strong and courageous. Do not be terrified; do not be discouraged, for the LORD your God will be with you wherever you go."

Joshua 24:14-15, "Now fear the LORD and serve him with all faithfulness. Throw away the gods your forefathers worshiped

Rising from the Ashes

beyond the River and in Egypt, and serve the LORD. But if serving the LORD seems undesirable to you, then choose for yourselves this day whom you will serve, whether the gods your forefathers served beyond the River, or the gods of the Amorites, in whose land you are living. But as for me and my household, we will serve the LORD."

What do you need to look for in a mentor?

Someone who knows what you have been through and how you can come out on the better side of life.

What can you learn from them?

How to arrange your life for victory and success by using a model that has worked well for them. I had a great one in a local guy named T. Fulton.

How can you serve them?

By being all in and taking on the tasks that are assigned to you and seeing it to the end.

Rising from the Ashes

How will you help someone as a mentor?

The best gift is to mentor someone else after you go through this process and it will give you unlimited rewards.

It is a natural response for people to help each other, yet many of us struggle with reaching out to one another. There are many passages in the Bible that address the issue of helping your brother. There is also scripture regarding not being afraid to seek help from your brother. Here are just a few of the passages that tell what the Bible has to say about helping those in need.

History

- From the beginning, God has wanted us to get involved and helping one another. In Genesis 14:14-16, Abram acts at once to rescue his nephew Lot when Lot is imprisoned. Sometimes we have to get into bad situations to help but that should not stop us from helping. We should act immediately to come to our brothers' aid.

Features

- One feature the Bible talks about regarding helping our brother is in Nehemiah 2:7-9. As well as helping our brother in his time of need, we should

Rising from the Ashes

be humble enough to seek help. Nehemiah prays to God for guidance about traveling to Jerusalem but he doesn't stop there. He also seeks help from other sources. You should never be afraid to seek out those people who are in a position to help you.

Considerations

- Matthew 12:10-12 talks about how the Pharisees were more concerned with human laws than being compassionate. They let their rules override the importance of helping others. They became upset with Jesus for healing someone on the Sabbath. Helping your brother in his time of need is more important than adhering to religious dogma. Luke 13:15-16 tells us that we should also not be hypocrites. You cannot pick and choose when you will help your brother. When God places the needy before us, we are obligated to help them.

Potential

- In Acts 2:44-45 the family the Bible says, "All the believers were together and had everything in common. Selling their possessions and goods, they gave to anyone as he had need." The family of God works better when its members work together. We should strive to help one another in our churches, as well as in our communities.

Rising from the Ashes

"At any moment, you have the ability to dramatically change any area of your life, or follow your heart's deepest desires. It's yours to create, any way you want it."
Craig Townsend

Rising from the Ashes

Health

To be able to get the most out of life and love it to its fullest, you have to have health that will help you in the long run as you work towards your goals and I would like to share the plan that helped me achieve the highest level of health possible in my life.

The Bible talks about meditation and its benefits as well; it was around long before the yoga practices.

NIV

Psalm 119:48

lift up my hands to your commands, which I love, and I meditate on your decrees

Psalm 1:2

Rising from the Ashes

But his delight is in the law of the LORD, and on his law he meditates day and night.

Genesis 24:63

Isaac went out to meditate in the field toward evening; and he lifted up his eyes and looked, and behold, camels were coming.

Joshua 1:8

Do not let this Book of the Law depart from your mouth; meditate on it day and night, so that you may be careful to do everything written in it. Then you will be prosperous and successful.

How am I going to live today in order to create the tomorrow I'm committed to? Tony Robbins

Rising from the Ashes

I firmly believe that any man's finest hour, the greatest fulfillment of all that he holds dear, is that moment when he has worked his heart out in a good cause and lies exhausted on the field of battle - victorious.
Vince Lombardi

Rising from the Ashes

I'm now a father to two wonderful kids.

Conner, who is a 6-year-old boy, is so full of life and has such a loving heart. He told me last year something that pushed me to write this book as I struggled to balance the checkbook for the business. He looked at me in his childlike manner and said, "Daddy, you don't have to work and worry about money. Just be who you are and do what you love and it will be taken care of." Wow, this was truly God using this little boy to relay his message to me.

Caroline is my little princess in the house who is now 21 months old and is the giggle box in the house. She's always laughing and giggling; she's such a joy with her head full of curls.

I have been blessed to have a special lady in my life who is also my wife Melodie, whose smile lights up a room and she helps keep me grounded and she is truly my soul mate as we have been together ten years now.

Rising from the Ashes

It's been her journey as well, as she stood by my side through it all when we had it all and when we had nothing. That is true love.

My mission is as follows:

To have the most positive impact on every person that I come into contact with and leave them in a better place than when I encountered them in life by allowing myself to be present, loving and nonjudgmental of their needs.

If winning isn't everything, why do they keep score?
Vince Lombardi

It's not whether you get knocked down, it's whether you get up.
Vince Lombardi

Give Gratitude Daily

Gratitude, thankfulness, gratefulness, or **appreciation** is a positive emotion or attitude in acknowledgment of a benefit that one has received or will receive.

Rising from the Ashes

Gratitude is an <u>extremely</u> <u>important</u> aspect of attracting to yourself the Abundance and Happiness that you desire and deserve in your life.

Gratitude Quotes to Live by

God gave you a gift of 86,400 seconds today.
Have you used one to say "thank you?"
~William A. War

Gratitude is an art of painting an adversity into a lovely picture. ~Kak Sri

If you have lived, take thankfully the past.
~John Dryden

As each day comes to us refreshed and anew, so does my gratitude renew itself daily. The breaking of the sun over the horizon is my grateful heart dawning upon a blessed world. ~Terri Guillemets

For each new morning with its light,
For rest and shelter of the night,
For health and food, for love and friends,

Rising from the Ashes

For everything Thy goodness sends.
~Ralph Waldo Emerson

"Gratitude is a quality similar to electricity: it must be produced and discharged and used up in order to exist at all." ~William Faulkner

"When you are grateful fear disappears and abundance appears"

Anthony Robbins

As I end this book I wish you much love and joy. Continue to strive toward your purpose in life and let nothing stand in your way of greatness that lies ahead waiting on you to claim it as your prized victory in life.

With Love

Rising from the Ashes

Billy J Brown Live with Purpose

Visit me at

www.billyjbrown.com

www.inspireyouproductions.com

I look forward to your success and wish you the best, and I ask you to send your success stories to me at

www.billyjbrown.com

Rising from the Ashes

Speacial Thanks to people and organizations that made a difference in my Life.

- Bay Community Church Malbis

- Shriners Hospitals

- Singing River Hospital

- Spanish Fort Church of Christ

- Baldwin County High Class 1990

- Jay High Class of 1990

- Anthony Robbins and Crew Members

- Bounds YMCA Staff and Members Daphne, Al

- Toastmasters Dist 77 all clubs and members

- Downtown Toastmasters Mobile, Al

- Starbucks which is where most this book was written.

Rising from the Ashes

-     Singers Mark Harris and Kirk Sullivan whose music inspired me when I wrote.

-     My Family members and many friends and the world of Facebook.

Great Reads that inspires me as well.

- Napoleen Hill Think of Grow Rich

- Donald trump and Robert Kiyosaki

  We want you to be

- Tony Robbins Awaken the Giant

- Dale Carnigie How to win friends and influence people.

Facebook:

Billy J Brown II Inspire You

Rising from the Ashes

At age Two prior to accident

Coaching my Sons team

Rising from the Ashes

My Great Family

Speaking to Group of High School Kids

Rising from the Ashes

My Joy in Life showing you to be your best !!!

Rising from the Ashes

To my Loving Wife

Rising from the Ashes

Be Blessed and Share your journey and story with me at

www.billyjbrown.com or

Billy J Brown Inspires you at Facebook

Live with Purpose!!!

Rising from the Ashes

Made in the USA
San Bernardino, CA
21 June 2017